The Holistic D

Introduction

As you have been drawn to this book I imagine you've felt a call to connect with the natural healing we can harvest from plants. In this book you will find information on a range of plants that can be offered to your dog through a self-selection process, allowing your dog to choose, to facilitate their own healing.

Working with the plants that grow around us teaches us to value them and is an integral part of living sustainably within our environment. Our most commonly used medicines have their origins in plants in the natural world. Plants now classed as weeds, such as nettle and dandelion, have been valuable healing allies for centuries.

Dogs have evolved to self-select plants which they require in their diet to rebalance their bodily systems, (homeostasis). They use their gut feeling, or intuitive sense, and their heightened sense of smell to self-select which plant material they need to heal themselves and therefore it is natural to consider adding plant material to your dog's daily diet.

The wonderful thing is that anyone can develop a relationship with nature regardless of where they live. You don't even need a garden as any small space, such as a sunny windowsill and collection of growing pots, can yield some wonderful ingredients to make home-made healing remedies.

There are a number of plants you can forage as opposed to grow in your garden. Rosehips, nettles and dandelions are good examples of this as they are plentiful and easy to identify. Foraging is the act of searching, identifying and collecting food resources in the wild. These include a wide range of plants, mushrooms, herbs and fruits growing around us uncultivated. Fortunately, we are blessed in the British Isles with a vast range of edible plants growing around us, not only in the forests but in our immediate surroundings. Chances are that these plants are growing on pathways you walk every day or in your local park. It is important to note that the everyday use of herbicides and pesticides can make any foraged food poisonous therefore be mindful of where you go to forage to ensure the plants are free from toxic substances. They are a whole range of books and courses that can teach you all about this amazing and rewarding pastime if you want to learn more.

Important Information

Contact your vet if your pet exhibits abnormal behaviour or has an illness. The advice outlined in this booklet is not an alternative to veterinary treatment. It is important to keep in mind that in the UK only a qualified vet is allowed to diagnose and prescribe treatment for an animal and this includes plant-based treatments. Aromatherapists, herbalists, homeopaths and flower remedy practitioners cannot legally diagnose and treat an animal with their remedies. However, as a pet owner, you are not prohibited from giving your own animal a plant-based remedy. As some plant-based remedies are contraindicated alongside certain health conditions or prescribed medication it is very important that you thoroughly research any plant-based remedy you wish to introduce to your pet and consult your vet for advice.

Instinct, Intuition and Self-Selection

Zoopharmacognosy is the scientific name given to the study of self-medication in the animal kingdom and how they self-select plants, soil and minerals in their natural environment to prevent and treat disease.

We can break down the term into the following 3 ancient Greek words:

Zoo – animal

Pharmaco – remedy

Gnosy – knowing

Many animals have evolved with an innate ability, (not learnt), to detect therapeutic constituents in plants and have created their own pharmacies from ingredients that commonly occur in nature. Using this innate instinct they know how to self-medicate and self-sooth. All animals and insects display this ability. Natural selection has honed a range of behavioural strategies that reduce physiological health threats from injury, poisons and pathogens. Animals differ in their dietary requirements and are capable of fine-tuning an optimal diet if they are provided with suitable choices. They do not need to 'know' what is missing from their diet in order to remedy that deficiency.

We naturally want to be the best dog parent we can be therefore it is important to consider incorporating choice into your dog's life. By watching what our dog chooses to eat, sniff and engage with can tell us a great deal about what is going on health-wise with them. While we often rely on logic they solely rely on instinct and intuition and we can learn a great deal from them by learning to tap into our own intuition which will always guide us to what our body needs to return to homeostasis.

Our dog's nose is fabulous and sees the world in smell-o-vision. Part of living with a dog is to recognise that a dog's sense of smell is important to them in a variety of ways. As owners we need to give our dogs time to sniff. It's not just their noses that are working, it's a large part of their brains too. Time spent sniffing can take the edge off excitable active dogs. For worried reactive dogs sniffing can help make them feel more secure as they have spent time working out what is out there and whether it needs to be worried about or if it is safe. For all dogs a chance to sniff fulfils a major part of their sensory needs. Sniffing makes them happy and gives them an outlet for their hard-wired natural behaviours.

Consider taking time each week to go out on a scent walk. Just let them spend the whole walk sniffing. Follow them wherever the scent leads. Watch your dog as they are doing this and try to understand how important scent is to them and consider what they may be discovering about the world. Also notice what plants they engage with, they may even nibble on some, which is a good sign that they need the nutrients within this plant introduced into their daily diet. There are some great smart phone apps available that can help identity plants when you are out and about on a walk.

Your dog's sense of smell is pretty much a superpower and their daily sniff routine can help them identify what's happening in their environment as well as lower their stress levels. Depending on the breed of dog their sense of smell is around 10,000 – 100,000 times better than ours. They possess up to 300 million olfactory receptors in their nose compared to about six million in ours and the part of their brain that analyses and processes scent is 40 times greater than our own.

Smell and taste are closely related and while a dog's sense of taste is a fraction of a humans their sense of smell is much more developed as they have many million more sensory glands in their nose than we do. Dogs can taste foods through their sense of smell with a special organ along their palate called the Jacobson organ. Dogs are generally not picky about the foods they eat but, if you do have a fussy eater, consider that dogs will more or less eat anything that smells good to them so choosing aromatic foods will increase your chance of success. As your dog ages so does his sense of smell. This can account for a declining appetite in some older dogs who are no longer able to smell food as well as they could when they were younger. You may find that a different food appeals to your aging dog because it has a stronger smell than what he's been eating. His sense of taste declines slightly too as he ages, but it's the sense of smell that sparks his interest and dictates what he wants to eat. This is an ideal time to introduce herbs to your dog's daily diet to encourage appetite and add the essential additional nutrients they may need at this time.

All dogs can be curious in the garden or out on a walk and it is useful to know which plants can be poisonous to our dogs to prevent toxicity. Different plants will flower during various times of the year, but it is important to remember it is not always the flower that can be toxic, bulbs and seeds can be toxic too. It is useful to be aware of poisonous garden plants throughout the seasons, particularly in relation to allowing self-selection.

Spring

Spring is a wonderful time of years where countless plants start to grow. Be particularly conscious where bulbs are emerging as some dogs may consider them food or a toy and they may be poisonous when eaten. The following spring plants will be harmful if consumed by dogs:

Apricots kernel, azalea, bluebells, buttercups, cyclamen root, daffodils/narcissus bulbs, elderberry, foxgloves, hyacinth bulbs, lupin, onion, rhododendron, rhubarb leaves, sweet pea stem, tulips, wild cherry tree, yew.

Summer

Be mindful when selecting plants, particularly if they are from a different climate. During the summer months, these plants may appear in higher numbers:

Deadly nightshade, foxgloves, lily of the valley, elder, hydrangea, geranium, ragwort, rhubarb leaves.

Autumn

The Autumn garden, pathways, local parks and the countryside provide dog walkers with the hazards of falling nuts, berries and leaves from trees and bushes onto the ground which are then sniffed, foraged and eaten. Plants to be mindful of are:

Acorns, hydrangeas, ivy, mushrooms and toadstools, fallen rotting apples, autumn crocus, chrysanthemum, conkers, oleander.

Winter

Though the number of visible plants decreases during winter, animal poisonings can still occur. Certain plants are bought into our home during the Christmas period and some of these are toxic to dogs. Beware of the following toxic plants:

Snowdrops, amaryllis, laurel, hippeastrum, holly, mistletoe and poinsettia.

What should I do if I think my pet has been poisoned?

If you think your dog has been poisoned by anything, you need to act quickly. Contact your vet as soon as your dog shows signs of being ill.

It's a good idea to write down the details of anything you think your dog has ingested, when they ate/drank it, how much they have swallowed, and what symptoms they have been experiencing.

If you have seen your dog eat something that they shouldn't, don't wait for symptoms to appear. Call your vet immediately and ask for their advice.

Therapeutic Plants and Flowers

Have you ever wondered which plants are the best ones to start growing in your animal healing garden but feel overwhelmed and don't know where to begin? Plants can be selected for a wide range of issues including supporting the digestive system, pain management, cell repair, immunity support, skin conditions and allergies to name but a few. There are so many great plants with an array of useful properties that you can grow with minimal gardening knowhow. I'm sharing with you my favourite selection of plants that you can choose to grow in your own animal healing garden to form the basis of many natural healing remedies for a range of aliments.

If you would prefer to buy dried herbs and flowers there are many good companies that can supply these herbs to you. As a general guideline 1 teaspoon of dried herbs is equivalent to 1 tablespoon of finely chopped fresh herbs. Try to use dried herbs that are less than 6 months old so they still have their potency.

Barley Grass *(Hordeum vulgare)*

Barley grass is a member of the grass family and the term barley grass refers to the young shoots of the plant before the stem itself has property developed before the plant produces grain. It is considered a superfood and has become popular as a nutritional supplement for humans and animals. Barley grass is rich in vitamins, minerals, protein, amino acids, chlorophyll and fibre. It is beneficial to a dog's digestive system as well as helping to boost its immune system. It can be offered fresh in a pot for your dog to nibble on or dried.

Barley grass is easy to grow in pots. Start in doors and sprinkle the seeds evenly across soil and cover loosely with soil. Place the pot in an area with indirect light and water daily but be careful to avoid overwatering. Harvest the grass at any point, use when it is about 6 inches tall for optimal nutritional benefits. Use scissors to cut the grass just above roots. Offer to you dog fresh or dry thoroughly and grind to use as a powder. You can let the grass grow a second blade for a second harvest however the nutritional content of grass from this will be much lower than grass from the first harvest.

Calendula *(Calendula officinalis)*

Calendula has antimicrobial, antibacterial, antiviral, antifungal and anti-inflammatory properties so it is an all-round super plant. It has significant healing properties for internal and external application and also a zesty flavour which makes it a useful culinary herb as well.

It can be offered orally as an infused oil to promote the soothing of the nervous system alongside enhancing the immune system. It is also a wonderful wound healer and skin-repair herb as it speeds up the healing of cuts, burns, and abrasions by promoting the formation of granulation tissue while preventing bacterial growth. Calendula tea is a highly effective wound wash or rinse and petals strained from freshly brewed tea make an effective poultice or wound dressing.

Native to Europe calendula is an annual that, once established, enthusiastically self-seeds and reappears year after year. To grow your own purchase seeds and plant them directly in the garden or start them indoors for transplanting after the last frost. Depending on your climate calendula will thrive in spring and early summer. For medicinal use look for traditional Calendula officinalis rather than modern hybrids. Calendula does best in full sun and any moderately fertile, well-drained garden soil. To avoid crowding thin the seedlings to between 4 and 6 inches apart.

Petals can be harvested throughout the growing season. They are sensitive to the weather and close up so always ensure you harvest the petals on warm sunny days when they are in full bloom.

Calendula is an annual and once the plants have completed blooming the seeds will fall to the ground. It is ideal to act before this happens to save the seeds for the following year. Wait until the flower has started to dry up and the petals are beginning to fall and remove the seed head. Lay the seed head in a cool, dry area to finish drying, shake the seeds out of the seed head and store them in a sealed glass jar or paper seed packets with the date of harvest and the name of the plant in a cool, dark, damp-free environment.

Chickweed *(Stelleria media)*

Chickweed is an annual plant that produces tiny white star-shaped flowers and has been used as a healing herb for centuries. All parts of the plant including stems, leaves and flowers can be used. It has anti-inflammatory soothing properties and is often selected as an infused oil to support with digestion and stomach upsets.

Chickweed is classed as a weed and a nuisance in the garden by many gardeners. Seeds are produced in large quantities with an individual plant able to produce 1300 seeds. It takes only 5-6 weeks from germination to seed dispersal and plants are capable of 4-5 generations per year so it can quickly take over a garden if not managed. Chickweed grows in any area of the garden, even in the shade, so it can be planted in any part of your herb garden but do be aware of its tendency to spread therefore it may be an option to plant in a large pot in an area away from the main garden. Before sowing soak the seeds in clean fresh water for around 12 hours for better germination and then sow the seeds directly onto the seed bed and cover with soil. The seeds germinate quickly and you can expect to see seeds sprout within a week or so.

Chickweed plants don't grow well if they are overcrowded so thin the seedlings by removing some of them when they reach around 5cms.

You can harvest the chickweed by snipping the top several inches of stems, leaves and flowers. Don't pull up the plants by the roots because it would prevent the plant from coming back the following season.

Comfrey *(Symphytum officinale)*

This healing plant has been used for over 2000 years as a herbal medicine for pain relief and is also known as' knitbone'. Its healing properties are, in part, due to the presence of allantoin. It can be made into an infused oil and applied over the femoral artery to support with sprains and swellings.

Comfrey is very easy to grow. Your local nursery will most likely sell comfrey as root pieces or crown offsets. Root pieces will take a little bit longer to get started than crowns, but both will grow equally well and should provide you with strong, healthy plants. You will only need a few pieces to get started because comfrey grows readily and is easy to propagate by division.

Start your roots or crowns in the spring. If you want, you can plant them directly in the garden once it is warm enough or you can start them ahead of time in pots indoors. If you start them indoors you can transplant them later into the place you want them to grow. It is possible to directly sow comfrey seeds however they may need up to two years to germinate, this is because they need a winter chilling to prepare the seeds to germinate. It is much easier and faster to grow comfrey from roots or crowns. When planting comfrey outdoors you'll want to space them at least two feet apart in all directions to allow them enough space to grow. If you are planting comfrey directly in the garden you'll want to wait until the danger of frost has passed. Comfrey is a tall plant with dainty bell-shaped flowers and therefore would do well placed at the back of your herb garden.

Make sure you wear gloves and long sleeves when harvesting comfrey because the plants can be a bit prickly and may cause irritation. As long as you leave a little bit of plant behind, you will have enough time to grow a second crop of comfrey in the same season.

Dandelions *(taraxacum officinale)*

Dandelions are part of the daisy family and a perennial plant. The entire body of a dandelion is edible. They are a rich source of vitamins C and A, potassium and iron. They act as an antioxidant, anti-inflammatory and boost the immune system.

Dandelions can be sown directly into containers or into the herb garden in early spring. They need to be thinned out once they have sprouted. They are easy to grow and do well in any soil however they do need full sun. They can go to seed within days of flowering and self-seed so be sure to clear the flowers before they bolt to avoid them taking over your garden.

A few weeks before harvesting the dandelions cover the plants with dark fabric to block out most of the light as this will blanch the leaves, reducing the plant's bitterness. The tender leaves can be picked throughout the growing season and will be less bitter than more mature leaves. Pick the flowers when they are their best in full bloom and place them directly into a bowl of cold water after picking to prevent them from closing up. You can harvest the roots at any time.

Dandelions can be eaten in just about any way you can think of. It is easy to make a nutritious broth that both you and your dog can enjoy, just add a few handfuls of dandelion greens, chopped carrots and pumpkin and a mix of dried herbs to

300ml of fresh vegetable stock and simmer until the vegetables are tender. The roots can be roasted at a high temperature for 10 mins and ground into a fine powder and a quarter teaspoon can be added to any food or drink.

Lavender *(Lavandula angustifolia)*

Lavender has anti-spasmodic and relaxant properties and is often selected by a dog needing comfort. It is also a natural insect repellent and is ideal for making into a hydrosol spray or infused rinse to use on your dog's coat and bedding.

English lavender and its hybrids are the hardiest types and can be left outside during winter in free-draining soil. They have a strong lavender scent, abundant purple or purple-blue flowers in summer and silver-grey leaves. Plants are widely available to buy during spring and summer in garden centres and online.

Plants are usually sold in containers ready for planting with the advantage that they can be transplanted with minimal root disturbance. Lavender is best planted in April or May as the soil naturally warms up and many fresh plants become available in garden centres. Lavender should never be planted in winter when young plants are vulnerable to rotting in cold, wet soils.

Lavender can also be planted in large containers. Plants in containers are always more susceptible to cold, as their roots are less insulated than when in the ground so be aware of this over the winter months. To help lavender survive move containers to a sheltered spot over winter, so they aren't exposed to really harsh weather.

Left to their own devices lavender can become woody and ungainly so, to keep plants compact and attractive, it's best to trim them annually in late summer, just after flowering has finished. Remove any spent flower stalks and about 2.5cm of leaf growth. You can easily make more lavender by taking softwood cuttings form young plants in early to midsummer. There is a wide range of different methods for taking cuttings, depending on the plant and time of year. Plants grown from cuttings will be identical to the parent plant.

Lemon Balm *(Melissa officinalis)*

Lemon balm contains a compound known as rosmarinic acid that has antioxidant and antimicrobial properties. Lemon balm can be used straight from the garden to keep your dog smelling fresh. Simply pick a few stems, crush the leaves, and run them over your dog's coat. In addition, lemon balm's citronella-like fragrance is said to repel mosquitoes and other insects. To make a lemon balm rinse, pour 1 cup of boiling water over 2 tablespoons of coarsely chopped fresh leaves. Cover and let stand until it cools to room temperature. After bathing your dog pour lemon balm tea all over as a final rinse to repel insects. Store leftover tea in the refrigerator in a spray bottle and use to spray your dog's coat and bedding. For best results, use within three or four days.

Lemon balm is a member of the mint family and has been revered as a medicinal plant for centuries. It is a bushy, leafy lemon-scented perennial herb. It is native to Southern Europe and its small white blossoms are so sweet they attract bees, hence the plant's scientific name, as Melissa is Greek for honeybee. When the plant is covered by bees it is a good sign it is ready to harvest.

The plants are easy to grow in almost any well-drained soil in either part shade or full sun. Sow seeds indoors from March to May in a small pot or tray of seed compost and cover with a thin layer of perlite or cover with a clear plastic bag and place in a warm spot or propagator. As soon as seedlings appear, which can take up to three weeks, prick out the seedlings into individual pots when they are large enough to handle. Transplant the young plants outdoors once all danger of frost has passed. Stems can reach 80cm tall so when planning your herb garden they are ideal to place near the back due to their height. Lemon balm can also be planted in large pots and also grown indoors. It needs a nice sunny spot with at least five hours of sunlight per day.

Pick fresh leaves as required throughout summer. Leaves for drying are best harvested before plants start to flower. Lemon balm is best harvested in the afternoon when its essential oils are strongest. The more it's trimmed, the more leaves it produces. Cut back after flowering to encourage a fresh flush of leaves and divide every few years in autumn to rejuvenate the plant.

Nettle (*Urtica dioica*)

Nettle is a fast-growing herbaceous perennial that is usually regarded as a weed but it is a wonderfully nutritious and beneficial plant to include in your herb garden. They are a superfood, rich in iron, vitamins A and D and packed with minerals. They are particularly useful to support the kidneys with detoxification.

Nettle thrives in full sun conditions but will tolerate some shade. It tolerates a wide range of pH levels, from very acidic to very alkaline. You will see new growth begin in February. Deadheading spent flowers will stop stinging nettle from spreading uncontrollably through self-seeding. Other than this no pruning is necessary other than pre-winter removal of dead stalks.

Nettles are easy to propagate simply by digging up plants from an existing patch and moving them to a new location. They are also easy to grow from seeds collected from existing plants. This is most often done with seeds collected from mature seed pods, stored for the winter, then sown indoors in seed trays six weeks or so before the last frost. The seeds are very tiny. Scatter them over the surface of a tray filled with ordinary potting mix. Press them lightly into the mix, and barely cover them with a bare sprinkling of soil as they need some light to germinate. Keep the tray lightly moist until the seeds sprout, which happens within about 14 days. The seedlings can be transplanted outdoors as soon as the soil is warm enough to be worked. No overwinter protection is needed, just cut back dead stalks in late autumn to prevent self-seeding in the garden.

While all parts of the nettle plant are edible the leaves and stems can't be eaten straight from the plant due to the barbs. Harvesting involves cutting back the top third of the plant, just above a node where leaves branch out, as this will encourage new growth. The leaves will have the best flavour for cooking if they are harvested before the plant flowers. The leaves of stinging nettle can be cooked and used in the same way as you would use spinach. Once dried nettles are safe to use. They can be used as a tea, infused oil or sprinkled as dry ground powder over your dog's food.

Parsley *(Petroselinum crispum)*

Parsley has diuretic, anti-bacterial, carminative and circulatory properties. It has been used as a medicinal herb for thousands of years and it is often self-selected for digestive issues, to remove excessive fluid build-up from the body and arthritis. It is also often selected by dogs who have been spayed. It can be offered orally as an infused oil to promote the soothing of the digestive system alongside supporting the urinary system and providing pain relief. Both the leaves and stems are highly nutritious and is an ideal fresh or dried herb to consider adding to homemade treats or to sprinkle over your dog's food.

Parsley is biennial, but usually grown as an annual, so sow fresh seeds every year for a continuous harvest. Sow outdoors from early spring to early summer into well-drained soil in sun or partial shade. Germination can be slow, taking up to six weeks. When the seedlings are large enough to handle, thin them out to 15cm apart. You can also grow parsley in large pots. Place in a cool, lightly shaded spot to germinate, and make sure the compost doesn't dry out.

Remove flowerheads to extend the cropping life of the plants throughout the growing season. If you don't have the time or space to grow your own plants from seed, you can buy potted plants in garden centres and supermarkets. These can be planted straight outdoors from spring onwards, into a sunny or partially shaded spot, in the ground or in a large container.

Peppermint *(Mentha x piperita)*

Peppermint has anti-bacterial, anti-spasmodic and decongestant properties and delivers cooling and pain relief to burns and itchy skin. It is a wonderfully versatile herb and can be offered as an infused oil for a range of illnesses affecting the gastrointestinal and respiratory systems. It can also be used as a cooling, soothing rinse for your dog's coat to relieve itchy skin, as a poultice/compress on burns and can be used as a cooking ingredient in homemade treats for fresh breath.

Peppermint needs lots of water and it is often found by streams and ponds where the soil is rich and the drainage is good. It won't tolerate dry conditions and while partial sun is sufficient for peppermint, planting it in full sun will increase the potency of its oils and medicinal qualities. It tends to spread and because of this it is useful to consider planting it in a pot.

If you're planning to grow your peppermint seeds indoors, you can start growing them at any time of year. Your house will be warm enough that the seeds will grow, even through winter. However, if you plant to grow your peppermint outside, the best time to plant is in the late spring. Peppermint can be grown anytime between the last frost of spring and 2 months before the first frost of Autumn. You can also begin growing seeds inside by sowing the seeds into small pots and keeping them warm and keep a lid over the container to hold the humidity in. Mist the inside of the container a few times a week and remove the cover when you notice the seeds sprouting, seeds will begin to sprout in about two weeks. Once you notice two true leaves develop on all your seedlings, it's time to harden them off.

At the end of the growing season prune off any dead flowers but leave a few of the flowers intact for later harvesting. Once they turn brown clip them and place them in a paper bag and leave in a cool, dry place until the flowers dry out. It will take around two weeks for the flowers to dry. Remove the flowers from the bag and crush them until they release their seeds. Blow any excess flower petals away with your breath and store in a sealed jar or seed packets in a cool, dark place until needed. Small portions of the plant can be potted up to overwinter indoors on a sunny windowsill to keep the supply of fresh leaves going until spring.

Roman Chamomile (*Chamaemelum nobile*)

Roman chamomile has anti-anxiety and anti-spasmodic properties which makes it a herb that dogs often select to address anxiety or compulsive behaviour along with stomach or skin disorders which are caused by the anxiety. Flavonoids, also found in Roman chamomile, are potent antioxidants with immune system benefits and anti-inflammatory properties. An infused chamomile tea can be added to your dog's food for them to benefit from its relaxing properties and calming effects on the digestive system.

Roman Chamomile is a perennial evergreen with finely divided, scented leaves and daisy-like flowers growing to a height of 20cm. It can be started from seed sown in late spring onto the surface of pots and cover with a thin layer of vermiculite so that the seeds are still visible as chamomile seeds need light to germinate. Place in a heated propagator to germinate and they should sprout in about two weeks. When seedlings are large enough to handle, prick out into individual pots. In spring plant out well-rooted seedlings or bought plants into light, well-drained soil in a sunny position or alternatively grow in pots. While it thrives outside chamomile will also grow very well indoors in a pot. It requires only four hours of sunlight a day so it can be grown throughout the winter if it has a spot by a sunny south facing window. Chamomile can become leggy unless it is clipped regularly during the growing season to ensure growth remains compact, dense and bushy. Gather newly opened flowers throughout summer. Regular picking will encourage further flowers.

Rosehips *(Rosa canina)*

All roses produce hips. Rosehips are full of vitamin C and antioxidants and can help strengthen the immune system. They can be offered in a powdered form to your dog mixed with a little oil or water.

Roses that grow in the wild form rosehips and you can forage for rosehips on rosebushes in the woods. You can also find wild roses growing on the side of the road in some areas. In your garden uncut rose stems will form rosehips. Don't remove all flowers when you prune your rosebushes. Leave some flowers in place so they can form rosehips after they mature. Harvest rosehips after the first light frost of the season passes as this helps sweeten the flavour. Plan to forage them in late autumn. You can harvest them earlier, but they will have less juice and be more bitter. Continue foraging for them throughout the winter.

After harvesting trim off the stem and blossom ends from the hip. Thoroughly rinse off the rose hips by running water over them in a colander. The hips can be used immediately or dried or frozen to be stored for future use. You can use whole, fresh rose hips, but the seeds inside have an irritating, hairy covering so it is best if you remove the seeds prior to eating. Cut the hips in half and manually scoop out the seeds.

Rosemary (*Rosmarinus officialis*)

Rosemary has anti-microbial, anti-oxidant, antibacterial and anti-microbial properties. Used as an infused water and rinse it helps with cuts and burns and helps repel fleas and ticks. It can also be ingested to support with internal infections, particularly infections in the digestive or urinary tracts.

Rosemary is a versatile herb, providing evergreen interest all year round. It thrives in a sunny, sheltered spot in well-drained soil. It can struggle in heavy clay soils, particularly in winter, when the ground tends to be wetter. You can grow rosemary in pots but it can become quite large and will need potting on in fresh compost every couple of years.

Rosemary is best started in the spring from ready-grown plants. Plant in a sunny, sheltered position in well-drained soil or grow in pots. Rosemary is an evergreen and can be harvested all year round. Cut back annually to prevent the plant from becoming woody. In cold winters bring plants under cover for protection. The soft new growths in summer have the best flavour. Snip off shoots as required, aiming to keep an attractive shape to the plant. As rosemary is an evergreen it's available fresh all year. It dries well but doesn't freeze. The leaves can be used fresh or dried for later use.

Valerian *(Valeriana officinalis)*

Valerian in an anxiolytic and sedative. It can be used as an infused water or hydrosol and stroked over the chest area or sprayed onto a cloth for the dog to use when needed.

Valerian is a hardy perennial and has been used for centuries as a healing plant for its calming effects. It will grow in a wide variety of conditions, from full sun to partial shade in well-draining soil and needs to be kept moist so water it frequently. Valerian can be grown from seed sown in spring, from softwood cuttings taken from new shoots in spring, or from established clumps divided in spring or autumn. Either sow seed directly where plants are to grow, in mid to late spring, or sow in containers under cover in early spring and grow on to plant outside in late spring to early summer. Valerian will also self-seed so you may find new plants turn up from one single plant growing in your garden. The plants grow to between 1-1.5m in height and produce white flowers so plant towards the middle or back of a border. After flowering in summer cut back faded flower stems to avoid self-seeding then cut back all growth after it has died back in autumn. It is the roots that are used for their healing properties which can be harvested in the autumn. The roots may take two growing seasons to be large enough to harvest. The plant will die back to the ground in winter but the roots should be fine and will put up new growth in spring.

When harvesting wash the roots thoroughly, removing the tiny fibrous roots around the outside, then dry in an airy place such as an outhouse or under cover outdoors, as the roots give off an unpleasant smell.

Yarrow *(Achillea millefolium)*

Yarrow is an anti-inflammatory and produces a cooling effect. It can be made into a salve, compress or poultice and used over the affected area to treat inflammatory pain, tissue damage and wounds.

The yarrow plant is a flowering perennial and blooms from June to September. Its stiff, flattened flower heads are made up of multiple tiny blossoms, some with contrasting centres. Start seeds indoors about six to eight weeks before the last frost date. Sow the seeds in moist, normal potting soil. The seeds should just barely be covered by the soil. Place the pot in a sunny warm location. The seeds should germinate in 14 to 21 days, depending on the conditions. They thrive in a wide variety of soils but do best in well-drained soil. Once planted it needs little care. It doesn't need to be fertilized and only needs to be watered during times of severe drought. Yarrow plants are vigorous growers and reach mature dimensions in the second year of growth. Prune the plant by about one-half after the first flush of flowers to keep the overall shape compact and encourage further blooming and harvest the flowers regularly when in full bloom throughout the growing season. Plants will die back and go dormant over the winter months.

Drying and Storage

There are a number of different ways to dry plant material:

- Bunch them together, tie with string, and hang in a warm, dry place for a few weeks, away from direct sunlight.
- Place them on a microwaveable plate and microwave on high for 3 minutes, stopping to turn the leaves at 30 second intervals. Never leave them in for the full three minutes without stopping as the leaves can burn or start a fire.

- Dry herbs in the oven by spreading onto an oven tray and drying on the lowest possible heat for 3-4 hours.
- Dry in a standard food dehydrator until crisp.

Like any other food plant material breaks down over time and start to lose their flavour once you grind them. If you're going to store ground herbs, make sure to do so in small amounts to avoid waste. Also, plant quality starts to disintegrate as soon as they're cut so if you're aiming for long-term storage, try to keep them intact for as long as you can. If they are too big for your airtight glass container, you next best option is to keep them in a vacuum-sealed bag.

Eventually, all plant material will reach the end of its shelf-life, but if you keep it away from certain elements you can extend that timeframe. Always keep track of how long you've had your plants for the best results. I always label and date the jar or bag.

Guidelines for storing dry plants:

Oxygen leads to breakdown over time, so it's best to store plant material in an airtight container. Glass jars and metal tins with screw-on lids are great as well as clamping lids.

Direct sunlight will degrade your dehydrated plant material, making it go stale faster. When left in the sun, dried plants lose some of their potency which directly affects their flavour and medicinal properties. Keep them in a closed cabinet or other dark area for best results.

Moisture is the enemy of any food storage and dried plant material is no different. If you dehydrate plant material yourself make sure that it is completely dry before storing. Even a single droplet of moisture can lead to mould growth which will ruin the entire jar.

The temperature where you store your herbs makes a huge difference. You don't have to keep them in a fridge or freezer but storing them at less than 75 degrees is best. Room temperature is fine, but many people prefer to store them in a cellar or a room that stays cool and at a consistent temperature throughout the year.

How to make Remedies for Common Conditions

Poultice

A poultice is a direct way to apply herbs to the skin. It is a simple preparation that can be used as herbal first aid and aftercare for burns, cuts and bruises, on joints to soothe injuries or arthritis, and for skin related conditions. Plants are usually crushed into a pulp or made into a paste that is spread directly onto the surface of the skin, up to an inch thick, and held in place with gauze or muslin wrapped around the area to keep the poultice from rubbing off. Adding a binder, such as clay, makes the poultice easier to apply and helps it stay put. Clay has its own skin-healing benefits as well and is especially helpful for drying weepy skin conditions. Poultices can be messy and an alternative version involves wrapping the moistened herbal material into a loose-weave permeable cloth before placing it on the area to be treated.

Infused Oil

- Select your plant material in relation to its properties and what you are going to be using it for.
- Sterilize a jar with screw top not rubber lid. Make sure it is bone dry.
- Put in plant material to just over halfway. The plant needs to be completely dry, if not once added to oil mildew may form.

- Add sunflower oil and leave an inch at the top to allow to breathe.
- I use sunflower oil as it is light, animals love it and it is easy to obtain. A heavy oil may take over the flavour of the plant.
- Put on the lid securely and shake it well.
- Put on window ledge for 8 weeks and shake well 2/3 times a week.
- After 8 weeks decant with a fine sieve and muslin a few times to make it as clear as possible.
- Label, date and store in a cool, dark place and use as required. Use within 3 months.

Basic Salve Recipe

You may choose to use some of your infused oil to make a simple salve. You will need 25ml of an herbal infused oil, 2.5g of beeswax and 2-5 drops of an essential oil, (optional).

Place the wax and infused oil into a bain-marie and mix together. Slowly heat the mixture until it has fully melted, do not allow to boil. Remove it from the heat and allow to cool slightly but not set. While still in liquid form stir in the essential oil, if using, and pout into a heat-resistant jar, place lid on securely and allow to cool.

Label, date and use within 3 months.

Hydrosol

A hydrosol can be created using equipment found in most kitchens and is really easy to make.

You'll need:

- A large saucepan with a well-fitting lid

- A heat resistant ramekin or another object a few inches tall.
- A heat resistant container to collect the condensed hydrosol.
- 1 large bunch of the herb of your choice.
- Water
- Ice cubes in a sealed bag
- A source of heat
- A sterilised container to store the hydrosol.

Method:

- Collect a dinner plate full of your chosen herb.
- In a large saucepan place an upturned ramekin or a similar object onto the bottom of the pan. You will add a heat resistant cup on the top of this to catch the water that will become the hydrosol.
- Arrange the plant material in the bottom of the pan around the ramekin.
- Add enough water to the saucepan to cover the plants. Put the heat resistant container on top of the ramekin. This will catch the hydrosol as it condenses at the top of the lid and drips back down.
- Invert a lid over the top of the pot. The most important part here is making sure there is a good seal between the pot and lid to limit the amount of steam that escapes. Turn the heat on to a low setting and bring the water to a simmer.
- When the water starts boiling, place ice in a bag (or an ice pack) on top of the lid. This will cool the steam and allow the water droplets to drop into the container below.
- Be prepared, this may take quite a bit of ice and will require a few refills of the ice bag until all the hydrosol is collected.
- Continue simmering until most of the water from the pot has been turned into a hydrosol and has collected in the container.

- When finished, pour the hydrosol from the container into a sterilized jar. Cool, seal, label and keep the hydrosol in the fridge for up to 7 days.

Herbal rinse/tea

It is so simple to make your own herbal tea or rinse using plants you have grown or collected yourself. Collect your plants straight from the garden, ensuring you do not remove more than one third of the entire plant. After rinsing dry thoroughly.

Make your preferred tea mixes by combining compatible flavours into a single bowl. Avoid crushing them to preserve the strong flavour. After mixing up your favourite blend put them into individual bags or airtight containers to preserve them. The mixes should last between six and twelve months. When you are ready to make a tea or rinse simply add boiling water, leave to stand for 5-10 minutes then strain or place a few teaspoons of leaves into a tea strainer. Use at least one teaspoon of dried herbs per cup of water, more to taste if you are making tea rather than a rinse. Use different variations of herbal mixes depending on the condition you are aiming to treat.

Home Made Remedies for Common Conditions

Arthritis / inflammation

Comfrey – offer as an infused oil or dried herb with a little water or dry.

Chamomile – offer as an infused tea.

Yarrow – apply as a salve or poultice over the inflamed area.

Peppermint – apply as a poultice, offer as an infused oil or make into treats.

Anxiety

Calendula – offer as an infused oil.

Lavender – make into a hydrosol and use on the coat and bedding.

Chamomile – offer as an infused tea.

Valerian - make into a hydrosol and use on coat and bedding.

Allergies / itchy skin

Lemon Balm - make into a hydrosol or infused rinse and spray over the coat.

Calendula - offer as an infused oil.

Lavender - make into a hydrosol or infused rinse and spray over the coat.

Peppermint - offer as an infused oil or apply as a rinse over the coat.

Immune System Support

Barley Grass – offer fresh straight from the garden or as a dried powder mixed with water.

Dandelion – make into a broth to offer alongside food, as a dried powder, whole fresh flowers or made into treats.

Nettle -offer as an infused oil, dried with a little water or make into treats.

Rosehips – offer whole/crushed or powered with a little water or oil.

Digestion

Peppermint - offer as an infused oil or make into treats.

Chickweed – offer as an infused oil.

Dandelion – make into a broth to offer alongside food, as a dried powder, whole fresh flowers or made into treats.

Parsley – offer dried with a little water or make into treats.

Coat and Skin

Calendula – offer as an infused oil for anxiety related skin conditions. Use in a salve on wounds and scar tissue.

Peppermint – use as a cooling rinse, as a salve on paws and ears and as an infused oil.

Yarrow – use in a salve or poultice over the area to be treated.

Nettle – use in a rinse for the coat, offer as an infused oil or make into treats.

How Plant Self-Selection Can Help Your Dog

Offering a range of natural plant-based remedies to your dog can help address:

- A physical issue
- A nutritional deficit
- Pain, inflammation or itching
- Detoxification
- Parasitic infestations
- Emotional issues

You can encourage your dog's innate skills or instincts for self-medication to create an experience to help address physical and emotional issues. By bringing this into your home it provides the environment to enable your dog to follow its instincts to heal and manage its health. This will stimulate their senses and instincts which, through their domestication, may have lain dormant. In the wild animals seek out what they need as soon as the sense their body going out of balance.

Our dog does not have the opportunity to do this, they are dependent on what we feed them or what they can forage from their restricted environments. They innately know what they need but have limited access. We often do not know there is a problem until symptoms appear and by this time the problem is well established and needs stronger remedies to put the body back into balance and bring it back to homeostasis.

You can test out the theories of plant self-selection by observing if your dog shows an instinct for selecting an appropriate remedy. Offer a range of remedies and allow your dog to self-select according to their immediate health needs. Your dog will show you what they need by selecting the appropriate remedies. They will only select what they need to re-balance themselves. It is also very useful to observe your dog when you go out on your daily walk if you walk in an area where they can forage as in this natural environment they may select grass to help them purge, chew on wood which may indicate a lack of fibre or eat herbivore or horse poo which may suggest a deficiency in gut flora. It is important to note that, unfortunately, a lot of natural foliage they might choose has been contaminated with chemicals which then make them unsuitable for selection.

The emphasis of any plant self-selection is based on choice. When considering how to use any holistic healing therapies for your dog the most helpful first step is to consider its immediate environment. Do they receive enough exercise? Are they on their own for long periods of time? Are you aware of how everyday household cleaning products can affect the health of your dog? Do you feed them the same food every day? Are they kept in a stressful environment? Is there tension in the household that can affect your dog's emotional well-being? There may be many things we can do to improve our dog's wellbeing on a daily basis just by considering and making adjustments to their immediate environment.

Humans can self-medicate but dogs are much more adept at it. We often crave certain nutrients during pregnancy, for example, or crave a fry-up to cure a hangover as our body needs salt and fluids. Each dog will have different needs and remedies selected along with the required dose needed will change each time, depending on what is needed on that particular day. It is very important that you do not project your own opinion of a remedy onto your dog as this will change their response to the remedy. Your dog mirrors your thoughts that you project onto it and, often, we can be unaware of this. It is important to focus solely on what your dog wants by allowing them to self-select the remedies they need.

Trust your intuition and trust your dog rather than just doing what someone else tells you to do. Having an in-dept knowledge of each remedy in terms of active constituents, therapeutic actions and any plant/drug interaction risks associated with it will be required to ensure you offer an appropriate selection. There are many scenarios where offering an animal the chance to use its self-selection skills is useful. Careful observational skills are key. Behavioural issues may sometimes indicate a physical root to their behavioural issues and by observing what is self-selected may lead to some surprising results. When dogs exhibit unusual chewing behaviour or eat non-food items they may be attempting to follow their innate self-medication instincts and this is a good time to offer a range of herbs, oils and clays.

Herbs, nutrients, essential oils. hydrosols (flora waters) and carrier oils are common remedies along with base materials including aloe vera, beeswax, clays and charcoal.

Herbs, Nutrients and Clays

Herbs and nutrients can be classed as any plants with a therapeutic action. They provide vitamins and minerals and are needed to assist in energy production, growth, repair and waste management. They cannot be stored for later use so are only selected when the animal needs them. They are selected when there is a deficiency/problem and the taste or smell changes when the correct dose has been achieved from pleasant/sweet to bitter if not needed. Allow you pet to select as much as they need and be ready to top-up the dish as needed.

It is a great idea to cultivate your own herb garden, is easy to do and maintain. It does not require a large space and many can be grown in pots on a patio or balcony.

When deciding which herbs to offer initially think if the animal originally evolved with this species of plant. If it did it is highly likely to be useful as a starting point when considering what to offer your pet. This is also an important point to consider when selecting clays. Clay or charcoal is selected when an animal needs to absorb toxins within the gut and to deactivate toxic compounds and poisons when they do not need them. Think about where in the world they originated from and what sort of clay would have been in that environment to know what to offer. For example, animals who would have had access to the seashore and sea are sometimes drawn to Dead Sea and green sea clays.

Herbs can be offered in fresh, dried or in powdered form and can also be made into an infusion or poultice. Powdered herbs are user friendly however only make in small batches ready to use as they lose their aromatic qualities quite quickly. You can make a powder by using a coffee grinder and then finish with a fine sieve.

Some popular examples of herbs and nutrients include barley grass, devils claw, liquorice, nettle, rosehip, seaweed and spirulina.

Herbs can be infused in a carrier oil. Carrier oils are fatty oils extracted from oil-yielding plants and each oil has its own unique set of therapeutic actions. Using carrier oils are to be avoided in dogs with pancreatic issues and only offer small amounts at any one time in healthy animals. Some to consider using are:

- Coconut: used as a purgative and/or externally as an antifungal
- Flaxseed: selected as an anti-parasitic and/or a laxative
- Hemp: improves the condition of the coat and supports dry skin

- Rice bran: improves the condition of the coat. Supports cardiovascular, nervous and immune systems. It is also self-selected to be used as a purgative
- Sunflower: used as a laxative and/or for parasitic infections.

Essential Oils

Animals have evolved with an instinct that drives them towards aromatic compounds and the aromatic volatile oils within plants. Essential oils offer a variety of therapeutic actions addressing physical, spiritual and emotional issues in animals. A wound of any kind holds the emotional memory of what caused it. Essential oils can be a very effective way to help release these emotions which may have been the underlying cause of the physical symptoms.

The lipid soluble nature of essential oils allows them to be more easily absorbed through the membranes in the mouth or skin. This route of administration will mean that fewer compounds are broken down by the liver and so more compounds are able to target the problem. Some can be toxic to certain animals and it is very important to fully research the effect that it can have and to avoid if in any doubt. Hydrosols or floral waters are a by-product of the steam distillation process used in the production of essential oils. They are mainly water and contain aromatic molecules from the plant. They are used undiluted and are mild and gentle. Essential oils can be offered via inhalation and some can be applied topically or licked off fingertips. When applying to the skin it is important to apply it over a gel such as aloe vera if the oil is an irritant.

When introducing essential oils to your dog:

- Always start slowly
- Allow your dog to self-select the oil.

- Introduce the oil initially with the cap ON as they have keen noses and a little goes a long way.
- Let them tell you 'yes' or 'no' by observing their responses and behaviour.
- Start out with the oil more diluted when introducing essential oils topically. You can increase the concentration if the desired effect is not reached.

Each dog is an individual and some may be more or less sensitive than others. You must allow your dog to take what it needs. Cutting a session short when they aren't ready to finish will do more harm than good and if you are using plant self-selection to support with pain this must be offering consistently and only once a week will not be enough.

Self-selection session guidance.

All animals, including dogs, have an innate system that detects a physical or emotional challenge such as stress, disease, injury or a nutritional deficiency. A lot of behavioural problems stem from physical issues so solving the physical illness will often help the emotional. Their body will release an internal signal in response such as a hormone or neurotransmitter. The animal will respond to these signals by seeking out remedies in response to the challenge they are facing. The animal will medicate on remedies until the signal ceases and the taste and smell preferences revert to normal.

A self-selection session can be valuable with regard to addressing nutritional deficits in your dog's diet. Herbs and essential oils help to facilitate food releasing energy. Most pet's diets are restricted in some way and can be lacking in essential nutrients. In the wild a wolf would feed on meat, seeds, berries, the whole of the animal they killed for food and plant content. A good diet is vital for energy, cell growth and reproduction, repair and waste management. Vitamins and minerals cannot be stored for later use, like fat stores from overeating, so they are selected as and when your dog needs them.

Dog owners often have a sixth sense about their dog's health and wellbeing and I would encourage you to trust yours. Using these instincts to select arrays of remedies for the issues you suspect can lead to very positive results. Dogs have an especially acute sense of smell, and due to the high volatility of the aromas, they reach a dog's olfactory sense very quickly. Each dog will respond differently to the volatiles and it may take a little while before you get a clear indication as to what is a 'yes' or 'no' response.

Session Setting

When conducting a self-selection session you want your dog to feel very calm and relaxed in an environment where it feels safe and happy, such as near his bed or by a sofa he can use. If the session is going to be carried out inside the room shouldn't be too small or your dog will be overwhelmed by the scents of the remedies. Keeping a window slightly ajar will help. If the room is too big a lead may be necessary at the beginning of the session until the dog becomes focused. In this case keep the lead held in a relaxed state so your dog can move away from the extract if needed.

Always aim to carry out the session when you are in a relaxed and calm state of mind. You and your dog share an energy bubble and they pick up on all of your emotions. If you are feeling stressed or in a hurry they will also feel these emotions and the session will not go well.

Session

If you go into a self-selection session with any expectations you will be putting pressure on your dog and they will sense this and the added pressure will affect their interactions. By not reacting to your dog's choices you will build their confidence to follow their instincts to reawaken the self-medication part of their brain.

Never force an extract on a dog and do not compare the intake of essential oil with macerates and other herbal remedies since they are a lot stronger. Let the dog guide the session and always make sure there is fresh water available. After dogs have selected oils for the bladder it is not uncommon for them to want to go outside to relieve themselves before continuing the session. Dogs with long noses and wolf dogs are very sensitive to smell and they may need to work near a window that is slightly open.

Positive responses

It is worth noting that dogs can take some time to give their positive or negative response to a remedy and, for a while, they may seem to ignore all the remedies after the first cursory investigation. Keep an open mind, try not to influence their behaviour in any way with your thoughts, and give them plenty of time. Signs of a positive response in dogs include:

- Yawning
- Standing still by the remedy
- Heavy eyes and/or blinking
- Lowering of the head
- Licking of lips
- Licking the air to catch the aromatics.
- A change in breathing pattern, or swallowing, puffing cheeks

- Agitated or excited behaviour followed by a spell of calm
- Alerting to a particular area on their body (looking at it, licking, gnawing or scratching at it).

Inhalation

If your dog selects an essential oil, allow the inhalation to occur at a distance to take into consideration their superior sense of smell. Begin by offering the essential oil approximately 10-30cm from your dog's nose, gradually bringing the bottle closer until the dog begins to turn its head way. Your dog may then choose to ease into a stronger dose so bringing the bottle a little closer and check. Your dog will keep approaching the scent or sniffing the air, all the while it is benefiting from the aroma, losing interest once it has had enough. Don't withdraw the essential oil too soon though, since dogs are prone to longer breaks between their keenness to smell the oils. If your dog jumps back in response to an aroma this means it has provoked a reaction and try the oil again later in the session. If the oil in question works on the mind, offer it again with other nurturing or calming oils.

Very often your dog will take a few sniffs, then turn away from the aroma and appear to be in thought. This can last from seconds to several minutes. When your dog returns to normal eye movement re-offer the remedy. Multiple sniffs at intervals allows the odour concentration to build up. Repeat this process until there is no further interest. If your dog's eyes follow the aroma when you take it away it means that the oil is not finished with. When there is no further interest go on to offer another extract.

At the end of the session re-offer all the oils that have provided the most interest to see which are most needed to continue with. Choose around six key remedies from the first session to work with until interest wanes. Other remedies may be needed in the days that follow. If there is prolonged interest in an oil offer it topically as a stronger dose may be required.

Topical

Many dogs appreciate a topical application of essential oils. You can apply a few drops of oil to your fingertips then stroke or massage your dog. The more you rub the essential oil between your fingers the weaker the dose. Offer a weakened dose first and this can be built up if required. The best therapeutic effects are achieved by applying the diluted essential oil to the femoral artery as the skin over this area is thin so access into the blood is fast. Dogs will sometimes stand and lift their leg for the oil to be applied here, a good way of them showing you what they need. Apply aloe vera to the site first before application as this will act as barrier and the skin will be less lightly to get irritated. Powered dry green clay can be applied after the oil to ensure that any oil that has not been absorbed gets mopped up and deactivated.

Do not use oils at the same time as any topical medications and avoid using cil on the nose, in the ears, in the eyes or around the genitals or anus of your dog.

Oral

When you and your dog are out on your favourite walk you might wish to use any herbs which grow along these walkways as part of the array you offer for a self-selection session. This will allow them to practise self-medication during their daily exercise too.

Powdered minerals, nutrients and herbs are generally licked. It is important to offer a choice of consistency between dry and wet. Barley grass and spirulina can have water splashed on them, leaving some area dry. Observe which is chosen. The medicinal herbs, such as liquorice root powder and devil's claw powder are mixed in a little oil, leaving a dry touch. Place all the selected herbal powders and nutrients in individual bowls on the floor at the same time. This allows your dog to alternate between the remedies to allow for greater absorption and the chance to be in control of their dosage as well as the rate it enters the body. Never add the remedy to their feed as you are taking the choice away from them and making the decision for them and they may not need the remedy.

Even though infused oils, such as comfrey can be invaluable, vegetable oils and infused oils should be avoided by dogs with pancreatitis. Also try to avoid or reduce them with overweight dogs and those with fatty lumps. Sometimes animals select a carrier oil to produce a purgative action and, in these cases, the dog might keep seeking out repeat doses. Dogs also choose carrier oils to aid conditions such as arthritis and other joint conditions in which case smaller doses tend to be consumed.

Essential oils are sometimes taken orally. In this case apply to fingertips as described above and offer to your dog, being mindful to increase the intensity of the dose gradually, until the correct strength is reached. Let your dog guide their dose and watch their reactions carefully.

Dose

If your dog shows a keen interest, or has responded to anti-bacterial oils, then offer the remedies as frequently as possible. Let them be your guide. Antibacterial and pain-relieving essential oils that are inhaled only will need to be offered more frequently or put out in inhalers. If applying over the femoral artery this may be done less frequent. Every dog and condition will be case sensitive and the frequency of offering the oils will vary. Some dogs may only require their remedies daily while others may initially need an hourly top up which will reduce over the following days. If the dog shows no further interest offer the remedies every other day, then weekly or monthly. If symptoms return re-offer the remedies.

End of session

Your dog will let you know when the session has come to an end by showing no further interest or distancing themselves from the extracts. They may go into a deep sleep or turn their back on you for a period of time. A lethargic dog may become more animated and playful. The aim is to leave your dog in a more balanced state. A full session may last up to two hours, with opportunities for your dog to rest and process their experience. Do not confuse processing with the end of the session.

The Toolkit

Herbs and essential oils contain multiple active constituents which, in turn, have multiple therapeutic actions associated with them. When you select a herb or oil to offer in a self-selection session for a specific identified condition there is plenty of scope to identify a possible different cause or complaint. Also, it is always worthwhile including a selection of behavioural and mood remedies as well as analgesic, anti-inflammatory and healing remedies. Even if you don't think your dog has any such issues they are prone to masking mood issues and injuries.

When using an essential oil on your dog's skin over the femoral artery it is advisable to apply a thin layer of aloe vera gel over the area first to act as a barrier should the oil be an irritant.

When offering oil on fingertips always rub your fingertips together first as this makes the essential oil weaker; the strength can always be increased over time if your pet shows an interest in the oil.

If your dog has pancreatitis infused oils should not be offered.

The Digestive System

The following remedies are useful to offer for conditions associated with your dog displaying digestive issues.

Basil essential oil: it is high in the constituents linalool and methyl chavicol and displays antidepressant, antimicrobial, antiseptic, analgesic, antispasmodic, carminative, digestive and nervine actions. As a digestive remedy, it may help digestive spasms, trapped wind, colic and bowel issues linked to nervous tension. As an antimicrobial, it may help in cases of digestive infections.

How to use basil essential oil: Inhalation, topical over the femoral artery

German chamomile (dried herb and essential oil): this is anti-inflammatory and anti-allergy and has the dual ability of soothing the digestive tract and the mind. It is a well-known sedative, relaxant, anxiolytic, nervine and soporific and is a key remedy for whenever digestive issues are caused or exacerbated by a nervous issue.

How to use German chamomile essential oil: Inhalation, topical over the femoral artery, oral on fingertips

Roman chamomile essential oil: this oil is analgesic, antimicrobial, antispasmodic, carminative, cholagogue, digestive, hepatic, sedative and stomachic. It is also a key remedy for digestive issues stemming from stress.

How to use Roman chamomile essential oil: Inhalation, topical stroked over the chest area

Green clay: this helps to mop up both toxins and excess acid. It will line and sooth the walls of the digestive tract.

How to use green clay: Clay can be licked dry or with water added. A self-selection session will show which they prefer.

Ginger essential oil: this is an antiemetic and it can do an effective job of easing feelings of nausea when inhaled. It can settle the stomach and pep up the digestive tract if it has become sluggish. It is also useful to note here that ginger is also very effective for travel sickness as it soothes the gut.

How to use ginger essential oil: Inhalation, topical over the femoral artery, oral on fingertips.

Marigold (Calendula) (dried herb): this herb is a soothing, anti-inflammatory remedy with an astringent action, which helps to ease diarrhoea. It is a popular choice when there is too much stomach acid that has led to irritation in the stomach and further down the tract. Marigold is also considered a good antimicrobial and antiparasitic and therefore may support an animal during infections. Ensure you have the correct English marigold (Calendula officinalis) and not the French type which is a different species.

How to use Calendula dried herb: Licked from fingertips or a small amount put down on a saucer.

Sweet orange essential oil: this is an antidepressant, antimicrobial, antiseptic, antispasmodic, carminative, cholagogue, digestive, sedative and a digestive tonic. Thanks to its uplifting nature, it is useful for digestive issues driven by problems with an animal's mood.

How to use sweet orange essential oil: Inhalation, topical over the femoral artery, oral on fingertips.

Peppermint essential oil: this potent oil has analgesic, antiseptic, astringent, carminative, cholagogue, hepatic, nervine, stimulant and stomachic actions. An important antispasmodic oil for digestive issues, peppermint also has a penetrating action on the mind.

How to use peppermint essential oil: Inhalation, topical over the femoral artery, oral on fingertips.

Alongside the essential oils you can offer a selection of nutritional supplements to your pet to aid their digestion and increase their antioxidants, vitamins and minerals in-take. These include spirulina dried powder, barley grass powder and rosehips. Offer each individually either mixed in a little oil, water or dry.

Constipation and Diarrhoea

Constipation and diarrhoea are two very common conditions. A constipated animal passes hard stools, often with decreased frequency, and very often it has trouble passing its motions. There are causes of constipation which requires a vet's treatment and it is therefore important to consult a vet about an animal's constipation first. Common causes of constipation include changes to their diet, a lack of bulking agents within their diet, dehydration, stress and/or a lack of mucus within the lower regions of their digestive tract.

Remedies to offer to a constipated dog include:

Flax or rice bran oil: these have lubricating and laxative actions.

How to use flax or rice bran oil: Licked from fingertips.

German chamomile essential oil: this has a regulatory action on the walls of the digestive tract, it soothes inflammation and it also acts on the nervous system, calming tension and anxiety.

How to use German chamomile essential oil: Inhalation, topical over the femoral artery, oral on fingertips

Prolonged or acute diarrhoea accompanied by other symptoms must always be investigated by a vet. It is common for an animal to experience the occasional mild bout of diarrhoea, indicating that something physical or emotional has temporarily upset its digestive tract. The following remedies can be offered:

Frankincense essential oil: this can address diarrhoea of nervous origin thanks to its calming and sedating actions.

How to use frankincense essential oil: Inhalation, topical stroked over the chest area

Ginger essential oil: this has a wonderfully settling effect on the digestive tract even through its scent alone.

How to use ginger essential oil: Inhalation, topical over the femoral artery, oral on fingertips.

Slippery elm powder: this contains polysaccharides which can sooth the gut.

How to use slippery elm powder: Offer dry or soaked in water.

Colic

Colic is the term used to describe abdominal pain in animals. It is a symptom rather than an illness itself. Colic can be caused by non-serious issues such as trapped wind and by mild microbial or parasitic infections, but it can also be a symptom of a much more serious issue. As always consult a vet first.

Remedies to offer in the case of colic include:

Green clay: this both absorbs toxins and soothes the lining of the digestive tract.

How to use green clay: Clay can be licked dry or with water added. A self-selection session will show what they prefer.

Fennel seed essential oil: this is a carminative and antispasmodic and can be a particularly effective remedy.

How to use fennel essential oil: Inhalation, topical over the femoral artery.

Roman and German chamomile essential oils: these are both carminative and have superb anxiolytic, relaxant effects. This calming activity is much needed for animals suffering from colic as they can become very distressed.

How to use German chamomile essential oil: Inhalation, topical over the femoral artery, oral on fingertips.

How to use Roman chamomile essential oil: Inhalation, topical stroked over the chest area.

The Respiratory System

Dogs can suffer from a range of illnesses that can settle in the respiratory tract. the aromatic volatile oils found in herbs and essential oils often have an affinity for this region. Inhaling potent aromatic compounds can exert useful antimicrobial, decongestant, expectorant and anti-inflammatory actions.

Some of the essential oils listed above are useful for respiratory illnesses, including the menthol-rich peppermint along with the anti-inflammatory and anti-allergy German chamomile. Other key, potent essential oils that can help breathe therapeutic actions through the respiratory tract are:

Clove essential oil: this has a potent spicy, sweet aroma that helps clear the airways and combat infections thanks to its eugenol content.

How to use clove essential oil: Inhalation, topical over the femoral artery.

Eucalyptus essential oi : this helps to open up and decongest the airways, whilst offering a broad-spectrum of antimicrobial activity.

How to use eucalyptus essential oil: Inhalation.

Frankincense essential oil: its action is penetrating and it helps an animal breathe deeply down into its lungs, all the while calming it with its relaxant effects. As an antimicrobial, it may also help to counter infection.

How to use frankincense essential oil: Inhalation, topical stroked over the chest area

Garlic essential oil: this is a potent decongestant and stimulates the white blood cells of the immune system, encouraging the resolution of respiratory infections.

How to use garlic essential oil: Inhalation, topical over the femoral artery.

Sandalwood essential oil: this oil has an affinity for the throat and inflammation, being a respiratory antiseptic and anti-inflammatory. It is a calming oil and can be very useful for calming the animal who becomes fraught by their respiratory illness.

How to use sandalwood essential oil: Inhalation, topical stroked over the chest area, oral on fingertips.

Aromatic herbs which can be offered up during respiratory issues in animals include:

Liquorice root: it's antimicrobial, demulcent, expectorant and anti-inflammatory actions are particularly useful.

Aniseed: this is a volatile oil-rich remedy which is effective in helping to reduce a cough.

Wild cherry bark: this is a very old expectorant remedy for coughs.

Marshmallow root or leaves: marshmallows are high in mucilage, soothing inflammation in the respiratory tract and helping to ease sore throats and coughs.

How to use aromatic herbs: Offer dry, as an infused oil or mixed in a self-selected oil or water.

Pain and Inflammation

In the wild animals become adept at hiding their injuries to protect themselves from predators. It isn't always easy to spot pain in an animal, unless that animal has a change of gait, is limping, or has some sort of visible injury. Internal pain may instead be expressed as restlessness or the animal may simply appear quiet, withdrawn or sleepy.

The alkaloids in passionflower offer analgesic activity and animals in pain will sometimes self-medicate with a carrier oil infused with this herb. The fact that this herb is also a superb relaxant and anxiolytic can be very beneficial when pain is distressing an animal.

How to use passionflower infused oil: Begin with 25ml, pause for a few minutes then offer again

Devil's claw is both analgesic and anti-inflammatory and can be used to ease the pain of musculoskeletal issues in dogs such as arthritis. Some dogs prefer this herb once it has been ground down to a powder. Due to its therapeutic volatile oil content, it is important not to keep the powder for too long or you risk losing its potency.

How to use devil's claw: Offer as a dry powder or mixed in a self-selected oil or water.

St John's wort is now a fairly well-known herb thanks to its efficacy as an antidepressant. It is also a good anti-inflammatory analgesic and one which animals often select when they are in pain. St John's wort is a specific remedy for nerve pain. This herb can be used in cases of arthritis, for musculoskeletal injuries, or when your dog has a toothache. St John's wort is best avoided if your dog is taking any prescribed medication due to this herb's drug-herb interaction concerns.

How to use St John's wort infused oil: Begin with 25ml, pause for a few minutes then offer again.

There are several particularly useful analgesic, essential oils used a self-selection session These are peppermint, German chamomile, Roman chamomile, lavender and yarrow.

How to use German chamomile essential oil: Inhalation, topical over the femoral artery, oral on fingertips.

How to use Roman chamomile essential oil: Inhalation, topical stroked over the chest area.

How to use lavender essential oil: Inhalation, topical stroked over the chest area

How to use yarrow essential oil: Inhalation, topical over the femoral artery, oral on fingertips.

When an animal is in pain, it can experience a lot of physical and mental tension, therefore introducing remedies which are a relaxant or sedative can be very useful.

Anti-inflammatory Remedies

Inflammation in animals, like pain, can sometimes be hidden by the animal. Tell-tale signs to look out for include swelling, heat and redness. Loss of function can occur as inflammation caused by the discomfort can restrict mobility.

Inflammation is a response initiated by the immune system and it serves a healing purpose. We often take anti-inflammatory medications to ease pain and speak of inflammation as a potential root cause of a range of health issues, but this mustn't lead us to view all inflammation as bad. Short-term inflammation in response to tissue damage is essential and it is only when the inflammation doesn't resolve that is becomes problematic.

Useful anti-inflammatories essential oils to include in the self-selection session are German chamomile, lavender, yarrow, peppermint, sandalwood, basil, black pepper, cinnamon leaf and ginger.

How to use German chamomile essential oil: Inhalation, topical over the femoral artery, oral on fingertips.

How to use lavender essential oil: Inhalation, topical stroked over the chest area.

How to use yarrow essential oil: Inhalation, topical over the femoral artery, oral on fingertips

How to use peppermint essential oil: Inhalation, topical over the femoral artery, oral on fingertips.

How to use sandalwood essential oil: Inhalation, topical stroked over the chest area, oral on fingertips.

How to use basil essential oil: Inhalation, topical over the femoral artery.

How to use cinnamon leaf essential oil: Inhalation, topical over the femoral artery.

How to use ginger essential oil: Inhalation, topical over the femoral artery, oral on fingertips.

Anti-inflammatory herbs that can be used topically include arnica as an arnica-infused oil. This is particularly helpful in cases of inflammatory arthritis. Lavender is a lovely soothing anti-inflammatory herb, which will calm your dog too, as well as easing pain. The analgesic St John's wort and Devil's claw mentioned above are both effective anti-inflammatories. Nettle can be used both internally and externally to address inflammation. If your dog has inflamed stiff joints you can pick nettles which you can then dry and infuse in a carrier oil.

How to use aromatic herbs: Offer dry, as an infused oil or mixed in a self-selected oil or water.

The Urinary System

When it comes to supporting animals through urinary problems the expertise of a vet is key. As an animal gets older incontinence can become an issue. In cases of incontinence, you might also like to offer your dog herbs which contain tannins, such as liquorice as an infused oil, as they may be drawn to these for their astringent actions.

Essential oils can aid urinary issues including inflammation and infections. Carrot seed, yarrow, juniper, patchouli and sandalwood essential oil can be offered in cases of cystitis. Offer mucilage-rich herbs too, such as marshmallow root or leaves as an infused oil, as these have been traditionally used to soothe the lining of the urinary tract in cases of urinary tract infections and inflammation.

How to use carrot essential oil: Inhalation, topical over the femoral artery.

How to use yarrow essential oil: Inhalation, topical over the femoral artery, oral on fingertips.

How to use juniper essential oil: Inhalation, topical over the femoral artery.

How to use patchouli essential oil: Inhalation, topical over the femoral artery

How to use sandalwood essential oil: Inhalation, topical stroked over the chest area, oral on fingertips.

Cuts and Grazes

Plant remedies with vulnerary, cicatrisant, cytophylacic, haemostatic, styptic, astringent and antiseptic properties are particularly useful when it comes to healing minor cuts and grazes. In the wild, animals are drawn to volatile oils, tannins and mucilages when it comes to addressing bleeding injuries and this is something you can keep in mind.

In terms of wound healing, you might like to offer essential oils or prepare an ointment used a dried herb. Essential oils to offer are lavender, German chamomile and yarrow. Healing antimicrobial essential oils such as rose may also be helpful.

How to use lavender essential oil: Inhalation, topical stroked over the chest area.

How to use German chamomile essential oil: Inhalation, topical over the femoral artery, oral on fingertips.

How to use yarrow essential oil: Inhalation, topical over the femoral artery, oral on fingertips.

How to use rose essential oil: Inhalation, topical stroked over the chest area, oral on fingertips.

Preparing a poultice is a useful way to apply many of the remedies, allowing them to sit on the skin for a prolonged period, exerting their healing effects. You can pound fresh herbs or dried herbs including lavender, calendula, plantain, German chamomile or yarrow plus a little water and then apply the paste to the area. This make-shift poultice strategy can be very cooling which many dogs like if their abrasion is hot or inflamed. Aloe vera is a soothing, cooling, anti-inflammatory gel when it comes to cuts and scrapes and can be applied directly to the wound site.

Just as clay is used by animals in the wild it can also be selected to be applied to the wounds of your dog. Either red or green clay can be used and, if blending the powder to a paste, you could opt to add a suitable herbal infusion or a healing hydrosol.

Burns

Aloe vera gel is a perfect carrier for essential oils and can be applied over the burn to reduce the heat. Yarrow and peppermint are both useful oils to use in aloe vera gel to treat the area.

Itchy Skin and Skin Infections

Antipruritic remedies such as chickweed infused oil licked from fingertips, peppermint or lavender essential oils and clay can all be used to tackle the symptoms of itchiness, which accompanies many skin conditions. When the itchiness arises from insect irritations offer citrus essential oils such as lemongrass or powdered neem.

How to use peppermint essential oil: Inhalation, topical over the femoral artery, oral on fingertips.

How to use lavender essential oil: Inhalation, topical over the femoral artery, oral on fingertips.

How to use lemongrass essential oil: Inhalation, topical over the femoral artery.

How to use powdered neem: Powdered neem can be dusted onto the coat.

Several fungal infections can irritate a dog's skin. Antifungal herbs, such as calendula, can be used as powders, ointments or, when made into infusions, as sprays or rinses. Clays, especially green clays, can be very soothing on the skin in cases of ringworm.

Parasites

Clays dusted onto the coat are a popular choice as are chickweed infused carrier oil, coconut carrier oil and sunflower oil offered on fingertips. Some animals eat grasses in an attempt to rid themselves of parasites such as worms, so allowing your pet opportunities to spend time among a variety of grasses may be useful.

Behavioural and Emotional Issues

Separation anxiety is a common issue for dogs left alone in the home when their owners are out at work. Dogs who have come from an abusive background, from a rescue centre or who have experienced trauma or a shock can also feel anxious and sad. In these situations the essential oils of neroli, lavender, rose, valerian and violet leaf are useful, as is orange blossom hydrosol. These remedies are all anxiolytic, relaxant and calming.

When a dog exhibits noise aversion, the essential oils of valerian, vetiver, frankincense, rose, neroli and lavender can be useful, as can rose hydrosol. These relaxing remedies can be used on nights when there are firework displays, to help adjust to a new baby/other dog entering the home or to adapt to a noisy road outside their home.

Some animals worry themselves to the point of exhaustion. This may be in the home when owners are out, on walks where they can become agitated by other dogs or when on a car journey. In these instances, the essential oils of rose, hops, valerian and violet leaf can be used to soothe anxiety.

A clever tactic is to use the remedy your dog has chosen when it is feeling relaxed, when being groomed, or cuddled/petted by you. Your dog will then start to associate that scent with feeling safe and relaxed and when that smell is used again the memory evoked will be a link to feelings of calm.

How to use neroli essential oil: Inhalation, topical over the femoral artery.

How to use lavender essential oil: Inhalation, topical over the femoral artery, ora on fingertips.

How to use rose essential oil: Inhalation, topical over the femoral artery, oral on fingertips

How to use valerian essential oil: Inhalation, topical over femoral artery.

How to use violet leaf essential oil: Inhalation, topical over the femoral artery or over chest area, oral on fingertips.

How to use orange blossom water: Spray in the air to create a comforting environment. Spray on bedding and over your hands when stroking your dog to help soothe them.

How to use frankincense essential oil: Inhalation, topical over the chest

How to use hops essential oil: Inhalation, topical over the chest

Anger and Dominant Behaviour

Calming these emotions with behavioural training alone can sometimes leave owners feeling overwhelmed and disheartened. Essential oils of hops, vetiver, ylang-ylang, sweet marjoram, rose, vanilla and valerian have all proved beneficial for calming down angry and dominant behaviour. The scents may need to be present throughout the day, rather than being used at certain points. Leaving a cloth out with a scent of the oil on it where your dog goes to relax or rest can be a good idea. Applying the scents to objects that your dog likes to play with, or take to bed, can also be very useful. Offering up habitat enrichment and boredom busters can also be beneficial.

Do's and Don'ts

Always contact your vet in the first instance if your dog exhibits abnormal behaviour or has an illness. A self-selection session is **not** an alternative to veterinary treatment.

Research your dog's health status and medications they are taking currently and ask your vet for advice before using any remedy.

Keep all remedies out of reach of children.

Always use the self-selection process and allow your dog to walk away from any application or remedy. Allow them to select extracts individually.

Use only therapeutic or medical grade essential oils.

Dilute essential oils prior to application topically. Use an aloe vera gel if using essential oils on delicate skin, especially with antibacterial and citrus oils.

Use caution with pregnant, nursing, or young dogs.

Understand the extracts you are working with and read up on how the remedy relates to the species you are working with.

Be careful where you put the bottles when not in use. Always replace the top, your dog may get hold of one while your back is turned.

Do not mix or add extracts to food otherwise it will interfere with the self-medicative process.

Do not apply large amounts of essential oil at any one time of offer a large number of oils at the same time.

Do not use a vaporiser / diffuser unless your dog can walk away from the aroma into another room.

Avoid offering vegetable and infused oils to your dog if they are prone to pancreatitis. Avoid or reduce with overweight dogs and those with fatty lumps. If concerned, consult your vet.

Avoid applying essential oils directly to stitches as they could dissolve.

Do not use water to remove an essential oil, rather dilute with a vegetable oil.

Make sure the undiluted essential oil does not touch their sensitive nostrils while offering an essential oil. Especially with irritants such as bitter almond, garlic and lemon.

Do not use essential oils around the genital area, on the nose, in the ears or in the eyes of your dog and avoid essential oil irritants.

Index of Therapeutic Actions

A

Analgesic – relieves pain

Anaesthetic – numbs, creates a loss of sensation

Anthelmintic – expels parasites

Antibacterial – kills bacteria or prevents their growth

Anticatarrhal – removes mucus from the body, from all body organs

Anticoagulant – thins the blood, reduces coagulation

Antidepressant – alleviates low mood and anxiety

Antidiarrheal – alleviates diarrhoea

Antiemetic – relieves nausea and vomiting

Antifungal – prevents and treats fungal infections, halts fungal growth

Antihistamine – prevents or reduces an allergic (inflammatory) reaction

Anti-inflammatory – prevents or alleviates inflammation

Anti-itch (antipruritic) – reduces itching

Antimicrobial – kills and prevents the growth of microbes

Antineuralgic – relieves pain derived from the nerves

Antirheumatic – alleviates symptoms of rheumatism

Antispasmodic – relaxes muscle spasms

Antitussive – prevents or alleviates a cough

Antiviral – prevents growth of or alleviates viral infections

Anxiolytic – reduces feelings and symptoms of anxiety

Astringent – contracts and tones mucous membranes and the skin

C

Carminative – prevents and expels intestinal gas

Cephalic – promotes blood flow to the head

Choleretic – stimulates bile production

Cicatrisant – promotes healing by stimulating scar tissue formation

Circulatory stimulant – boosts the circulation

Cooling – its use promotes a cooling sensation on the skin

Cytophylactic – promotes the growth of new cells

D

Decongestant – alleviates congestion in the nasal passages and airways

Demulcent – soothing, relieves irritation

Diaphoretic – promotes sweating and can help manage a fever

Digestive – aids the digestive system

Diuretic – increases urine production

E

Emmenagogue – promotes circulation to the pelvis and uterus; stimulates menstruation

Emollient – softens and soothes the skin

Expectorant – helps the lungs bring up mucus, makes a cough productive

F

Febrifuge – reduces a fever

G

Galactagogue – promotes milk flow

H

Haemostatic – stops bleeding

Hepatic – benefits the liver

Hypnotic – calms, soothes

Hypotensive – decreases blood pressure

I

Immunostimulant – stimulates the activity of the immune system

L

Laxative – encourages peristalsis and bowel movements

Lymphatic – stimulates the lymphatic system

N

Nervine – nourishes the nervous system, calms and balances

R

Relaxant – calms and relaxes

Rubefacient – promotes blood flow to the skin

S

Sedative – calms and sedates

Stimulant – stimulants the mind or body

Styptic – stops bleeding

Sudorific – promotes sweating

T

Tonic – restores health in general or has an affinity for a particular organ

U

Uterine – improves the function of the uterus

V

Vasodilator – dilates blood vessels

Vulnerary – promotes wound healing

By working your way through this book you have equipped yourself with a great deal of information regarding plant self-selection. I do hope you have enjoyed learning more about this fascinating subject and feel inspired to grow a few of your own healing herbs and flowers. Let this booklet serve to remind us that nature still has much to teach those of us who are willing to watch and learn.

If you want to learn more about plant self-selection visit the website for details on our plant self-selection course:

www.animalhealingtherapies.co.uk/courses

I hope you come to love all aspects of healing and plant self-selection as much as I do.

To learn more and get in touch:

Visit the website: www.animalhealingtherapies.co.uk

Email me: alison@animalhealingtherapies.co.uk

Printed in Great Britain
by Amazon

40751797R00066